TAKE A MOMENT

Beating teenage depression & Anxiety

A workbook

Brook Waters

Copyright ©2018 Brook Waters

Published by Teen Life Skillz

www.TeenLifeSkillz.wordpress.com

TeenLifeSkillz@gmail.com

All rights reserved. No part of this book shall be reproduced, stored in a retrieval system, or transmitted by any means, electronic, mechanical, photocopying or otherwise, without express permission of the author.

ISBN-13: 978-1717195609

ISBN-10: 1717195601

Dedication

This book is for YOU
You are worth it
You CAN do this
You may have days where it doesn't feel possible
But HOLD ON
It WILL get better

Contents

How to Use this Book 9
    About this Book 10
    Using this Workbook 11
    Chill Time 12

My Safety Plan 13
    Emergency contacts 14
    Current Medication 15
    Safety Plan 16
    My Emotional Thermometer 19
    Fun Page 20

Depression 21
    Being Depressed 22
    Getting Help 25

About Me 27
    About Me 28
    Who am I? 29
    My Coat of Arms 30
    How Do I Feel Now? 31
    Where I Am Now 32
    Where I'd Like to Be 33
    People I Trust – My Team 34
    Definitely Not on My Team 35
    Chill Time 36

Coping Strategies 37
    Strategies for Coping 38
    My Favorite Treats 40
    My Favorite Healthy Food 41
    My Favorite Exercise 43
    Things I Like Doing 45
    Fun Page 46

Fight, Flight or Freeze 47
Fight Flight or Freeze 48
How Our Reactions Work 50
Strategies 51
Relax 52
Create Active Experiences 53
Create Active Experiences 54
My Active Experiences Mind Map 56
My Quiet Activities 57
My Quiet Activities 58
My Quiet Activities – Mind Map 60
More About Me 61
Places I Like 62
Music That Makes Me Feel Good 63
Books/ TV Shows / Movies I Like 64
How I Express Happiness & Excitement 65
Chill Time 66
Build an Emotional Thermometer 67
What's an Emotional Thermometer? 68
Your Scoring System 70
What affects you? 71
Triggers & Hazards List 72
Example: Emotional Thermometer 73
Another Emotional Thermometer 74
Fun Page – Your Own Design 76
Build a Sensory Box 77
Build a Sensory Box 78
Things for My Sensory Box – Mind Map 81
Things for My Sensory Box — List 82
Be a Warrior 83
Being True to Yourself 84
Things that Make Me Sad 85
Safe Ways I Can Express Sadness 86

Things that Make Me Angry	87
Safe Ways I Can Express Anger	88
Saying Yes and No	89
Everyday Things I Don't Like	90
Everyday Things I Like	91
Warrior Shields	92
My Warrior Shield	93
Design your own shield from scratch	94
My Treasure Chest of Memories	**95**
What's a Treasure Chest of Memories?	96
Nice Things That Have Happened Lately	97
My Favorite Memories	98
Cool Times with Friends	99
Just For Fun	100
Build a Sticky Note Wall	**101**
What's a Sticky Note Wall?	102
Lyrics / Quotes that Mean Something	103
Qualities I Like About Myself	104
Things I'm Good At	105
Cool Things Others Say About Me	106
Cool Things I Say About Others	107
Chill Time	108
Work Your Plan	**109**
You Can Do This	110
Tracking Progress	**111**
My Mood Log	112
My Medication History	116
My Medication History	117
Where I Am Now	118
Where I'd Like to Be	119
Where I Am Now	120
Where I'd Like to Be	121
Safety Plan	122
Safety Plan	124

    Another Word Find 126
More Resources 127
    Online Resources 128
    Emotional Thermometer 129
    More Coloring Pages 130
    More Sudoku 132
    Another Maze 134
    Good Luck and Good Planning 135

How to Use this Book

About this Book

This book is not a guide to depression or a diagnostic tool. It wasn't written by a psychologist or a team of researchers. This book contains techniques used every day by teenagers who are battling depression—and winning!

Depression is different for everyone. This is a practical workbook to help you figure out who can help you and the type of strategies that work for you—even on your worst days. Using this book, you can make positive safety plans that suit you.

But it only works if you open it and start writing, drawing and dreaming your way through the pages. It might take a little time, but it will be worth it. YOU are worth it. YOU can do this.

This journal will help you plan for great days and combat the bad ones.

May you find nuggets of joy on your journey.

Using this Workbook

Use Your Ideas to Build a Plan for Bad Days

Throughout this workbook, there are activities designed to feed into your safety plan and give you resources to use on a bad day. Collect up ideas and transfer them to your plan as you go. There's a safety plan at the front of the book, and extra blank plans in the More Resources section at the back. You don't have to do everything in this book. Use the parts that work best for you.

Ideas from teenagers for teenagers

Teenagers with anxiety and depression gave truckloads of input in developing this workbook. They use many of these activities to help them through the bad times. The fun & chill pages were their idea too. They hope you enjoy them too!

Write, draw or mind map

We're all different. Some of us love to draw, while others cringe at seeing our own doodles on paper. Some love writing and making lists, and others prefer mind maps. Some love a blank page, but for others it's a nightmare.

Use these pages however you want—doodle all over the cover, the margins, and across the lists if you want to. Or fill the drawing pages with writing. Do whatever your thing is!

That's what this book is about—discovering what you love and what works for you.

Flip through the book and have a look before you start, so you're comfortable with the structure and know where things are. You don't have to use the whole book, just what suits you.

Once you've had a sneak preview, fill in the emergency contacts on page 14, and then start at page 21. But first, it's chill time!

Chill Time

Find your way through Bob's head. It's busy in there—don't get lost!

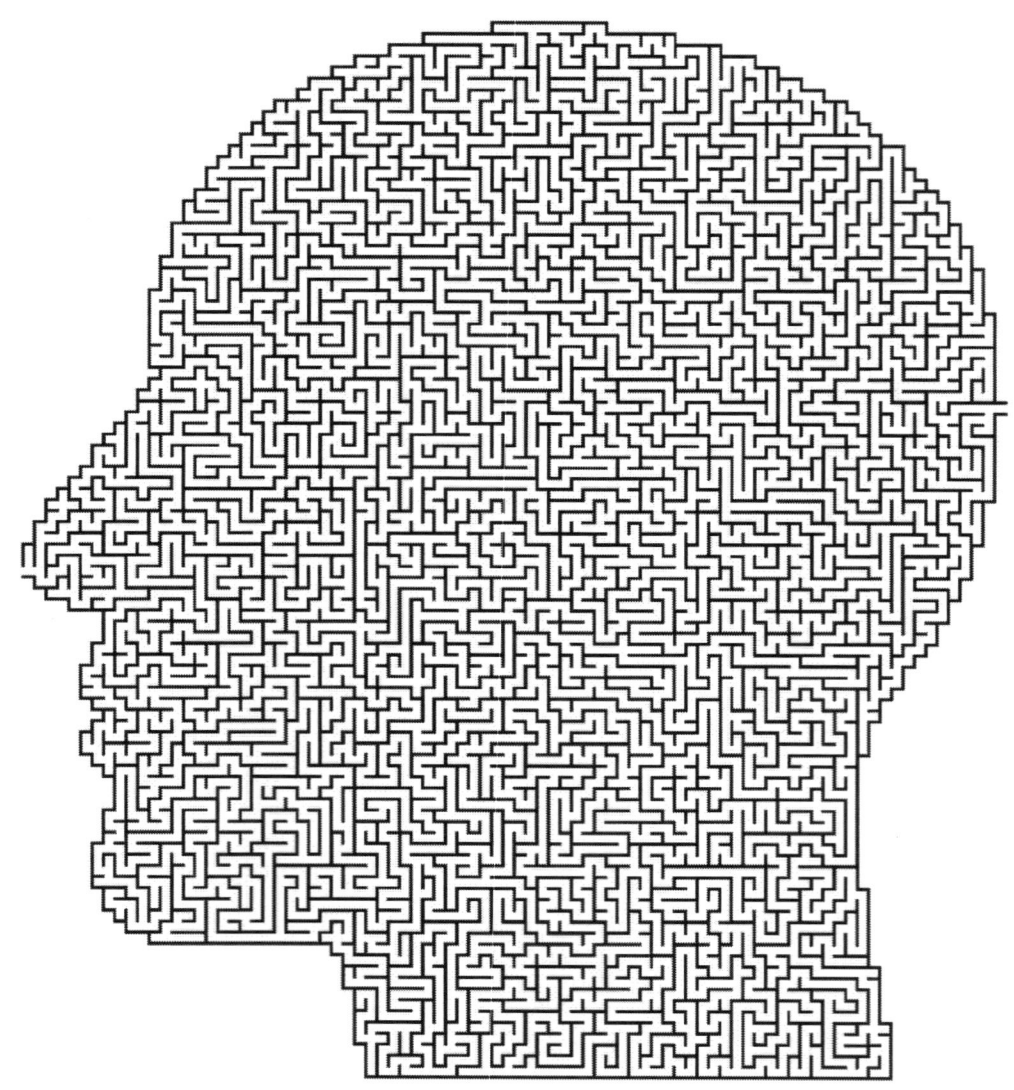

Life can be a maze, but there's usually a way through.

My Safety Plan

Emergency contacts

Psychiatrist's Name:	
Phone:	
Email:	
Psychologist's Name:	
Phone:	
Email:	
Consultant's Name:	
Phone:	
Email:	
Doctor / GP's Name:	
Phone:	
Email:	
After Hours* Contact:	
Phone:	
Email:	
Pharmacy Name:	
Phone:	
Email:	
Local Emergency Room:	
Phone:	
Email:	
Personal Contact 1 Name:	
Phone:	
Email:	
Address:	
Personal Contact 2 Name:	
Phone:	
Email:	
Address:	

* After hours contact may be the hotline for the organization that takes care of you, or the hospital's after hours psychiatry team, or another hotline.

Current Medication

Medicine	Start Date	Dose Time/s & How*	How I feel	Side Effects	Date Stopped Why?

* Note the dosage, when it should be taken and any special instructions, e.g.: take with food, or one hour before sleep etc.

Safety Plan

(Work your way through this book and fill in your plan)

When I feel desperate, I'll talk to or be with (pages 25, 26, 34 or 38):

_____ Phone:_____

_____ Phone:_____

_____ Phone:_____

_____ Phone:_____

_____ Phone:_____

Places I can be safe (from page 62):

_____

_____

_____

_____

Things I'll do (including things from: quiet activities, pgs 58-60; active experiences, pgs 54-56; friends, pgs 34, 38; things you like to do, pg 45; safe things you can do if you're angry or sad pgs 86, 88).

_____

_____

_____

_____

_____

_____

_____

_____

_____

Things I'll take with me (including: sensory box, pgs 78-82; treasure chest of memories, pgs 96-99; this workbook; favourite distractions, pg 64; music, pg 63; food, pg 40-41; phone; medication pg 15 etc):

_____

_____

_____

_____

_____

Other Safe Ideas:

My Emotional Thermometer

(copy this from page 75 or 76)

Fun Page

Have fun finding your way through this one.

Depression

Being Depressed

If you feel sad, angry, resentful, anxious or have a low mood for longer than a couple of weeks, then you may have depression. If it has gone on for a lot longer, then get help immediately. Everyone's different, so depression comes in as many shapes, shades and colors as we do. Here are some common causes of depression.

Reactive Depression

Depression can be caused by an event that makes us sad. Sadness is natural and only becomes depression when it continues for more than a few weeks.

These events (and others) can cause depression:
- someone dying
- a relationship break-up
- war
- losing a job
- illness
- alcohol or drug abuse
- loneliness
- accidents
- having a baby (postnatal depression)
- trauma
- bullying
- physical or emotional abuse
- sexual abuse
- family history of depression
- less sunshine hours (seasonal affected disorder or SAD)
- a radical change in your life

Clinical depression

Depression can also be caused by an imbalance in chemicals in the brain. Neurotransmitters, or chemical messengers, help regulate your mood. Endorphins, dopamine, norepinephrine and serotonin help us feel happy, sleep well and maintain a healthy appetite. If these chemicals aren't present in the right quantities, then your mood will continue to be low. It's a tough cycle: if you feel low, then the 'feel-good chemicals' in your brain aren't released, which leads to further low moods. It's important to get medical help.

Virus-driven depression

In the last few years, several studies have investigated the effect of viral or bacterial infections on depression. If your depression occurred at the same time as a major infection or illness, discuss this with your doctor.

Unhelpful Advice

We've all heard people say things like:
- Stop moping
- Look on the bright side
- Stop being so sad
- Don't be a glass half-empty person
- Snap out of it
- Pull yourself together
- Have a little faith
- What's your problem?
- There are many people worse off than you
- Think happy thoughts
- It's all in your head
- Cheer up!

While people mean well with these types of comments, they don't actually help. What helps is having someone understand you, listen to you, and support you so you can take action that will lift your mood, help you see a brighter future, and help you take care of yourself today. Your doctor will ensure you get that sort of help. If your doctor doesn't understand, seek another doctor who does.

Don't Stay Stuck

When you realize you're depressed, that's the time to act. Reach out and tell someone. Get help. If you haven't told anyone yet, see your doctor as soon as possible. If you want, take a friend or support person with you. Waiting usually prolongs your recovery.

Big Black Scary Secret

Sometimes depression can feel like a dark, scary secret. We can feel ashamed that 'we're not handling it', that we can't 'snap out of it' or 'cheer up'. However, if we have a broken leg, we need treatment. We don't keep walking on it and saying, "I'm fine." Depression is a condition that needs treatment too. You deserve to feel better, to have enjoyment and happiness in your life. No one is happy all the time, but if, most days, you're sad, angry or distressed, then you need support to recover.

Recovery

Understanding what causes your depression helps you know what situations are likely to affect you. This helps you plan strategies to manage your mental health. It isn't an easy journey. Depression is complex, and you'll probably need help to figure it out. While this workbook isn't intended to help you understand the cause of your depression, it will give you some insights into your behavior and help you identify strategies for managing your mental health.

Statistics

Statistics show that people who have depression and get help, recover much faster than those who don't get any support. Once you have help, depression becomes much more manageable. Don't stay stuck—get help!

You can do this!

Getting Help

The first step is to tell someone who can help you.

Family

Sometimes, family relationships can be difficult or even cause depression (if they're dysfunctional). However there are often family members you can reach out to. Is your mom or dad supportive? Do you have an understanding caregiver or guardian? Do you have an uncle, aunt, cousin or favorite grandparent who will listen? Do you have older adult brothers and sisters who can help?

Friends

As teenagers we often have friends who love to help us. If you're unable to tell a family member how you feel, it may be easier to confide in a friend. However, depression is an issue that's bigger than just 'sharing with a friend,' so please get your friends to support you in getting help from an adult who knows what services are available.

School

At high school, there are many people available to help with depression. You could talk to a guidance counselor, home-room teacher, dean, your favorite teacher or a deputy principal. Some schools have school nurses or visiting health professionals. Take a friend for support and go and see someone. If they don't understand, try another person until you get the help you need.

Medical Professionals

Your doctor is a great place to start. If you're unable to afford a visit to the doctor, then some community health organizations offer free services to teenagers.

Your doctor may refer you to a counselor, psychologist, psychiatrist or an organization that deals with mental health issues. These people are experienced and trustworthy and deal with many teenagers with depression. They'll understand you and be able to help. Most teens find relief in dealing with professionals who 'get it'.

Organizations

Your doctor, teacher or the guidance counselor at school should be able to put you in touch with a local organization that can help. You may end up speaking to a social worker or a medical professional (see above). If you're stuck, look online and see what free services are available from local organizations that support teenagers with depression or anxiety. If you can't find anything, call a hotline or a helpline, and ask them what's available.

Medication and Natural Alternatives

Antidepressants are often prescribed for depression when it's been longstanding. There are many different types of antidepressants and it's essential to seek medical advice to make sure you receive the right type.

In addition, a lot of research has been done on natural supplements. There is some research that supports omega 3 (found in fish oil) and B vitamins as aids to staying mentally healthy.

There are also a whole range of supplements that are sold over the counter for helping mood, HOWEVER, it's really important to get medical advice before taking them as some of these react badly with anti-depressant medication and in some cases you need to stay off supplements for a few weeks before starting anti-depressants. Most psychiatrists are aware of these supplements and keep up with the latest research, so do seek medical advice before taking anything.

Online resources

There is a list of online resources at the back of this workbook. As well as seeking online help, there are local help lines you can call.

About Me

About Me

This is a title page, all about you.

If you like drawing, draw a picture of yourself here.

If drawing's not your thing, glue in a photo or use words.

Who am I?

My Name:	
My name/s mean/s:	
What I like about my name:	
What I don't like about my name:	
My favourite name:	
Why?	
My favourite animal & why?	
My favourite activities & why?	

My Coat of Arms

Use your favourite things from the previous page to create a coat of arms with your new name, favourite color, animal and activities.

Have fun!

How Do I Feel Now?

Today's date __11-03-20__

My favourite color:

| Yellow |

I feel like this color now:

| |

My favourite weather:

| Sunny |

I feel like this weather:

| Sunny |

My favourite emotion:

| happy |

I feel like this now:

| relieved |

Stuff that happened today (why I feel this way):

Where I Am Now

Date: 11-03-20

		Low High
Mental	Mood:	1 2 3 4 5 6 7 8 (9) 10
Mental	Studies/School:	1 2 3 4 5 6 7 8 9 (10)
Mental	Being Creative:	1 2 3 4 5 (6) 7 8 9 10
Physical	Physical Health:	1 2 3 (4) 5 6 7 8 9 10
Physical	Time Outside:	1 2 3 4 (5) 6 7 8 9 10
Physical	Eating Habits:	1 2 3 4 5 6 7 8 9 (10)
Physical	Water Drinking:	1 2 3 4 (5) 6 7 8 9 10
Physical	Exercise:	1 2 3 4 5 6 7 (8) 9 10
Social	Family:	1 2 3 4 5 6 7 8 9 (10)
Social	Friends:	1 2 3 4 5 6 7 8 9 (10)
Social	Relationships:	(1) 2 3 4 5 6 7 8 9 10
Social	Having Fun:	1 2 3 4 5 6 7 (8) 9 10
Spiritual / Mental	My Purpose:	1 2 3 4 5 6 7 8 (9) 10
Spiritual / Mental	My Past:	1 2 3 (4) 5 6 7 8 9 10
Spiritual / Mental	My Present:	1 2 3 4 5 6 7 (8) 9 10
Spiritual / Mental	My Future:	1 2 3 4 5 6 7 8 9 (10)

Draw an arrow to show which direction things are moving.
This gives you a baseline for later.

Where I'd Like to Be

When? __7 weeks__   08-04-20

		Low									High
Mental	Mood:	1	2	3	4	5	6	7	8	9	**(10)**
	Studies/School:	1	2	3	4	5	6	7	8	9	**(10)**
	Being Creative:	1	2	3	4	5	6	7	8	9	**(10)**
Physical	Physical Health:	1	2	3	4	5	6	7	8	9	**(10)**
	Time Outside:	1	2	3	4	5	6	7	8	9	**(10)**
	Eating Habits:	1	2	3	4	5	6	7	8	9	**(10)**
	Water Drinking:	1	2	3	4	5	6	7	8	9	**(10)**
	Exercise:	1	2	3	4	5	6	7	8	9	**(10)**
Social	Family:	1	2	3	4	5	6	7	8	9	**(10)**
	Friends:	1	2	3	4	5	6	7	8	9	**(10)**
	Relationships:	**(1)**	2	3	4	5	6	7	8	9	**(10)**
	Having Fun:	1	2	3	4	5	6	7	8	9	**(10)**
Spiritual / Mental	My Purpose:	1	2	3	4	5	6	7	8	9	**(10)**
	My Past:	1	2	3	4	5	6	7	8	9	**(10)**
	My Present:	1	2	3	4	5	6	7	8	9	**(10)**
	My Future:	1	2	3	4	5	6	7	8	9	**(10)**

There are more of these charts at the back of the book in the More Resources section.

People I Trust – My Team

Add to this list as your team grows. Add these names to your plan.

Name	Why I like them
Doggo	Fluffy

Definitely Not on My Team

(You can use code names for these people, if you like)

Name	Why Not?
Josh Wilko	Idot
Jo Sweazer	Idot
Ryan FS	Just Ryan

Chill Time

If you enjoy Sudoku, take a break.

5	3			7				
6			1	9	5			
	9	8					6	
8				6				3
4			8		3			1
7				2				6
	6					2	8	
			4	1	9			5
				8			7	9

Coping Strategies

Strategies for Coping

Being Honest

One of the most important strategies when you're depressed is to find people you can be honest with about how you feel. These may be:

- close friends
- your favorite teacher
- a guidance counselor
- your doctor
- psychologist
- psychiatrist
- your mom, dad, caregiver or guardian
- nurse
- uncle, aunt, cousin or other relative
- granddad or grandma
- social worker
- someone from a helpline or a support organization

It could be anyone else you know who has your best interests at heart and will support you in getting help.

If you can't think of anyone, go back to your lists:

- People I trust, on page 34
- Getting help, on page 25

And put the names of people you can be honest with on your safety plan (page 13) under the section 'I'll talk to'. If there isn't anyone yet, reach out and get help.

Get Back to Basics

To take care of our mental health, we also need to take care of our bodies. This can be challenging, especially if we don't feel very positive about ourselves. We need a few basics to keep ticking along—eating well, sleeping, drinking water, exercise, relaxation and fun time with friends.

Eating

Often depression leads to a decrease in appetite. Sometimes we eat food high in sugar, fat or carbohydrates (junk food such as chocolate, potato chips etc) or sugary or stimulating drinks (soft drinks, energy drinks, caffeine). Most of these substitutes for healthy food give us a short term artificial boost, and then make us feel worse.

Try to eat healthy food wherever possible. If you don't have much appetite at all, try eating small healthy snacks regularly e.g.: half an apple, a banana, some nuts, a small lunch that includes protein and vegetables, e.g.: cheese and crackers, carrots and dip etc. If you have chronic weight loss or gain due to eating disorders, medication or lack of appetite, then see your doctor as soon as possible.

Go to My Favorite Healthy Food and Favorite Treats over the page and brainstorm. Prepare your lunch or snack, knowing this food will help you feel better in the long term.
Treats are good to have too. It doesn't all have to be healthy, it's just important to have a balance. So enjoy listing your favorite treats as well.

Drinking Water

Our bodies are two thirds water. Water plays an important role in carrying nutrients to our cells and carrying away our wastes. Dehydration—not having enough fluid in your body—can cause headaches, fatigue, grumpiness and poor concentration. It also affects your sports performance. Female teens should drink 5-6 glasses per day and males should drink 6-7 glasses of water a day. Adults should have 8-10 glasses.

My Favorite Treats

(Write, draw or mind-map here)

TITAN

My Favorite Healthy Food

(Write, draw or mind-map here)

LETTUCE

Sleep

Regular sleep patterns help us regulate our moods. However, depression and anxiety can disrupt your sleep, so sleep deprivation can be a vicious cycle. Having a bed time routine can help settle you more so you're likely to sleep. Try playing music you like, reading a book, being in a calm space and going to bed at the same regular time. Relaxation exercises (page 58) may also help.

If you have chronic sleep issues, such as nightmares or night terrors, problems getting to sleep (regularly longer than 30-40 minutes), waking throughout the night or other sleep disturbances, then please contact your doctor or mental health team. There are many strategies to help sleep deprivation. Your doctor can help you find what suits you best. It may take time, so be patient.

I know one teen who had only slept 3-5 hours a night, for four years. His psychiatrist has just found a combination of therapy, exercise and medication that has reduced his bad dreams, helped him fall asleep faster and stay asleep. It has taken them 10 months to find the solution and his sleep isn't perfect, but it is a lot better. Now that his sleep has improved, it's helping his mood. If you want to track your sleep patterns, you can log your sleep on the mood log in the More Resources section.

Exercise

Regular exercise can boost your mood by increasing the feel-good chemicals in your brain. Doing the type of exercise you enjoy will help you do it more often. If you don't enjoy exercise, then try some new types of exercise until you find one you do like.

Some ideas: fencing, biking, boxing, gymnastics, swimming, mountain biking, skateboarding, walking, skipping, jumping on cardboard boxes, dancing, cross-country running, athletics, football, basketball, cricket, baseball, yoga, Feldenkries, horse riding, stretching, Pilates, aqua fitness, aqua jogging, diving, line dancing, ballet, kayaking, water polo, underwater hockey or trampolining. See a sports teacher to find something that suits you.

My Favorite Exercise

(Write, draw or mind-map here)

Horse Riding
Park Run
Hiking

Relaxation

Relaxation techniques help lower your distress by dropping your adrenaline levels, and decreasing panic and anxiety. Learning effective relaxation techniques will help you find more calm moments in your day. We'll talk more about adrenaline and relaxation in the next section, and again in My Quiet Activities.

Relaxing is an important part of taking care of you. Take time to chill. Find out what you enjoy doing that calms you down and helps you have mental space. Some of your favorite activities may be active, like skating, drawing or composing a tune. Other activities may be more passive, like watching a movie or listening to music. What do you enjoy? How do you relax? List them on the next page.

Time with Friends

Spending time with friends can also help you to unwind and have an enjoyable time. What sort of things do you enjoy doing with friends? Do you bike? Watch movies? Game? Play in a band? Just talk?

If you find being with some friends has a negative effect on you, then think about who else you know. It's your choice. You can choose people that help you feel good. Or you can choose relationships that are destructive. Honest friends who help you feel good are going to help you more in the long term. List what you enjoy doing with friends on the next page.

Avoiding Harm

One of the basic ways of taking care of yourself is to avoid harm. Avoid substance abuse. Don't take illegal drugs, or abuse medicines. Don't smoke or drink alcohol. Most of these substances are depressants. Alcohol, for example, makes you feel good for a few minutes, then acts as a depressant, lowering your mood further than it was. It affects your judgment, often leading to bad choices and can also lead to long term depression. We'll discuss emotional hazards and triggers in the section, Your Emotional Thermometer.

Take care of you. You are important.

Things I Like Doing

Add some to your plan

Sleeping
Netflix
Cadets
Horse Riding
Photo tings
fashion

Fun Page

If you like words, take a quick trip into outer space!

D	H	O	B	S	H	N	E	P	T	U	N	E	Y
U	E	J	I	H	U	N	Y	S	T	H	A	O	R
D	N	A	U	U	E	E	E	M	A	E	N	W	A
W	N	A	I	P	L	U	T	O	N	A	D	O	H
A	G	H	P	L	I	Z	O	O	E	R	U	S	U
R	D	E	I	H	C	T	M	N	W	T	N	S	H
F	H	Y	H	O	P	B	E	O	Q	H	I	U	E
R	A	C	O	E	A	A	R	R	T	E	O	A	E
U	S	A	T	U	R	N	C	P	L	A	N	E	T
R	T	A	E	H	F	T	U	E	U	L	E	E	E
I	E	U	C	U	F	A	R	O	V	C	E	I	O
A	R	F	A	I	R	A	Y	A	O	E	I	R	H
T	O	A	I	N	I	A	B	E	A	R	N	A	E
O	I	E	T	E	O	E	N	A	A	E	H	U	A
E	D	I	D	D	O	E	D	U	T	S	E	T	S
E	S	Z	E	E	H	O	P	H	S	L	U	M	S

VENUS
EARTH
MARS
CERES
ASTEROIDS
JUPITER
SATURN
NEPTUNE
URANUS
PLUTO
DWARF
PLANET
MOON

Fight, Flight or Freeze

Fight Flight or Freeze

How We Think

How we think determines how we react to situations.

If we're hiding from an enemy and someone taps us on the shoulder, then we leap out of our skin. If we're relaxing with a group of good friends and someone taps us on the shoulder, we're more likely to turn and see who it is.

If we're in a safe environment, we're more likely to react in a positive way. If we're in a danger zone, we'll react with fear. Our brains are clever. They store up our past experiences and reactions, so we have information about how to react in the future.

If you're in a terrible accident with sirens wailing, next time you hear a siren, you're likely to have a negative reaction because your subconscious remembers the accident. But if you had a birthday party with rides in a police car, with sirens and all as a kid, you may associate sirens with happy times.

Stage performance is another good example of an experience that can be both positive and negative. Being on stage can be exhilarating and terrifying. Some people feel one of these emotions, others feel both. It depends what we believe.

Excitement and Fear

Excitement and fear can be different sides to the same coin. Take our friend about to perform on stage. If she's feeling great about being on stage, her heartbeat is raised, she's alert and ready to react and her body is flooded with adrenaline. She's excited. If she's terrified, she has the same physical reaction—raised heartbeat, adrenaline, alert and ready to act—but she's anxious and stressed out.

The physical reactions to excitement or fear are similar. It's what we think, or our belief system, that influences our emotional response.

Belief system

Our belief systems are made up of past experiences, things we've been told and a complex mix of the cultural and family messages we grew up with. Our state of mind also influences our belief system. Having depression, post-traumatic stress disorder (PTSD), anxiety or panic attacks, also influences how we react.

By looking at your belief system, and figuring out what things have influenced you, you can decrease your anxiety. It's hard work, but it's worth it. Help is available from therapists and counselors.

Our Protective Reactions

There are a few common reactions to stress:
- Flight (run away and avoid stress)
- Fight (hyped up on adrenaline, ready for action)
- Freeze (paralyzed by fear or anxiety)

Things that create our automatic negative feelings are called triggers. We each have personal triggers. We'll talk about these more in the Emotional Thermometer section.

If we recognize our triggers, we can plan strategies for managing our negative reactions and reducing the strength of our reactions. Having a plan helps us to focus and not panic.

Fight

When we're full of adrenaline, ready to fight, we need activities that allow us to release our energy in a positive way.

Flight or Freeze

When we're filled with anxiety, we need activities that calm us. We'll look at these soon. First, let's take a look at how this all works.

How Our Reactions Work

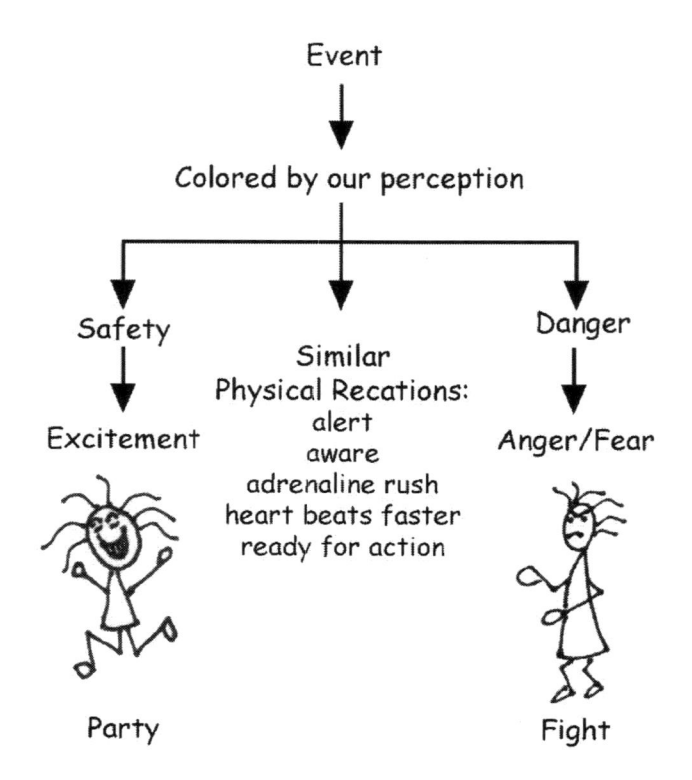

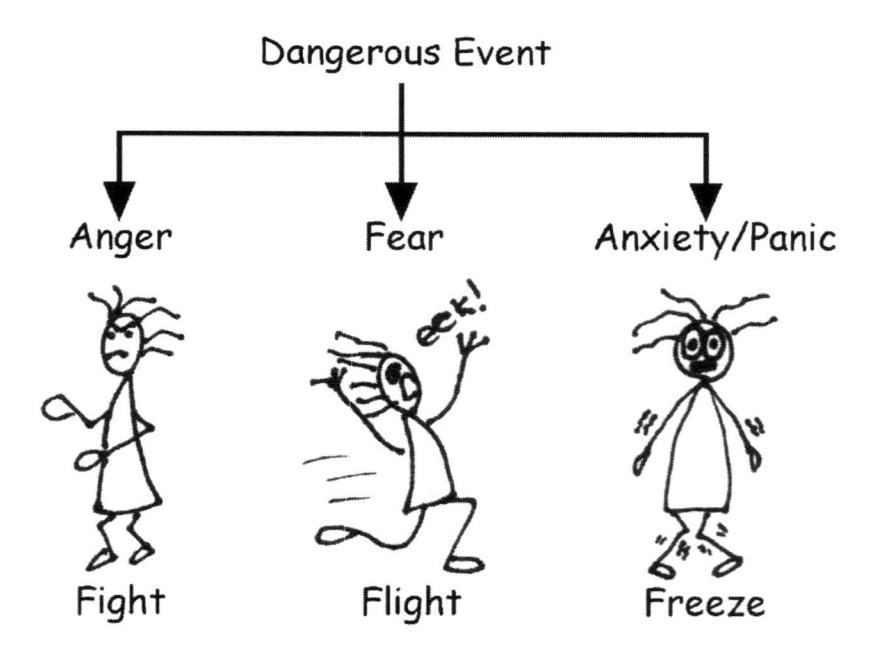

Event

↓

Colored by our perception

↓ ↓ ↓

Safety → Excitement

Similar Physical Reactions:
alert
aware
adrenaline rush
heart beats faster
ready for action

Danger → Anger/Fear

Party

Fight

Dangerous Event

↓ ↓ ↓

Anger — Fear — Anxiety/Panic

Fight — Flight — Freeze

Strategies

Being proactive is a big part of feeling in control, even when your thoughts are spiraling and negative. By developing lists of strategies, you'll have options when you get in a tough situation. Remember that there are three types of activities:
- Activities that release energy (most effective for fight state)
- Activities that make you calmer (useful for flight or freeze states)
- Activities that distract you (useful for all 3 states)

The great news is that you can choose what works best for you, and you can use all three types of activities. The following sections will help you plan activities that will work for you.

- Emotional thermometer (awareness of what you react to)
- Scales for measuring emotions
- Quiet / calming activities / relaxation techniques
- Treasure chest of memories
- Sensory box
- Active experiences (that release energy)
- Safe ways to express anger
- Safe ways to express sadness
- Exercise
- Music

As you work your way through this workbook, you'll create lists and mind maps of strategies that work for you. Add them to your plan at the front of the book, and remember, no plan is set in concrete. You can always change things as you go. Keep what works. Ditch what doesn't! The freedom to choose is yours.

You <u>can</u> do this.

Relax

Coloring time!

Create Active Experiences

Create Active Experiences

Our hormones kick in when we experience strong negative reactions, pumping adrenaline around our bodies in a *fight or flight* reaction. When we're distressed, angry or fearful, being active can help us process the adrenaline and feel better. Studies have shown that most people process their emotions better while they're doing something physical.

If you make a list of active experiences, when you're distressed you can use these activities in your safety plan. Here are some activities teenagers have done to help them with sadness, anger, rejection or hurt. Tick the checkboxes if you like them.

- ☐ Splatter paint on paper
- ☐ Pop bubble wrap
- ☐ Jump on bubble wrap
- ☐ Go to the gym
- ☐ Write your feelings on paper and rip it into tiny pieces
- ☐ Roll a newspaper and hit the floor with it until the newspaper is in tatters. Then make another one.
- ☐ Squash or rip old cardboard boxes.
- ☐ Take a shower or bath (hot/cold)
- ☐ Rub ice cubes on your arms
- ☐ Smash ice (freeze water in 1-2L plastic containers)
- ☐ Graffiti photos of people in old magazines
- ☐ Re-live a happy moment (use your treasure chest of memories)
- ☐ Sing or play a musical instrument
- ☐ Eat a chili pepper
- ☐ Reorganize your room
- ☐ Get a friend to drive you to a deserted place and scream in the car. (Please don't distress anyone who's around. Let them know you're playing)
- ☐ Hug pillows and soft toys

- ☐ Squeeze ice
- ☐ Run your hands under cold or warm water
- ☐ Snap a rubber band against your wrist
- ☐ Punch cushions
- ☐ Run on the beach, in a forest, or at a park
- ☐ Sprint as hard as you can
- ☐ Visit a playground and enjoy the little kids' equipment
- ☐ Kick a soccer ball against a wall
- ☐ Hammer a piece of wood (with a friend, to stay safe)
- ☐ Run up and down flights of stairs (slowly on the way down)
- ☐ Play with sand or kinetic sand
- ☐ Smash polystyrene into a box (& clean up all the bits)
- ☐ Yell into a storm
- ☐ Go on a bike ride with a friend
- ☐ Draw or paint a picture
- ☐ Dance vigorously to your favorite music
- ☐ Cuddle a pet
- ☐ Go on swing
- ☐ Write a poem or a song
- ☐ Write the lyrics to a song on your arm with a whiteboard marker
- ☐ Learn to sing/play or memorize your favorite song
- ☐ Play the drums on a cushion (with fake drumsticks if you don't have any)

What now?

Have fun designing your own activities on the next page. Use these to safely express sadness, hurt or anger (see pages 86 & 88).

My Active Experiences Mind Map

(Write, draw or mind-map your activities here)

Add some of these to your safety plan

My Quiet Activities

My Quiet Activities

Relaxation/Calming Techniques

Sometimes when we're distressed, quiet time often helps us to calm down. We need to go to a safe place, or be with someone safe, and then use relaxation or meditation techniques to calm our thoughts. Here are some examples:

- ☐ Quiet Breathing: Lie in a dark, quiet room and breathe slowly. Breathe in on three counts, hold your breath for three counts, and then breathe out on three counts. Focus on your breath. Repeat until you feel calm.
- ☐ Visualize a safe place where you like to be. Feel your feet in that place (e.g.: in sand, earth, water or a soft carpet). Feel your body there, (e.g.: lying in warm sand, floating on water, on a soft bed, in a field etc). Hear and feel the surrounding environment (e.g.: babble of water, birds calling, the swish of wings overhead, sunshine on your face). Relax and breathe deeply.
- ☐ Repeat positive affirmations about yourself in your mind. Or write out positive things about yourself.
- ☐ Listen to relaxing music
- ☐ Progressive muscle relaxation: Lie in a quiet place. Tense your left foot and feel the muscles bunch, then relax it and feel how everything goes soft. Do the same with your calf, then thigh. Progress to the right side of your body, then work your way up your torso, down your arms and then your face, tensing and relaxing each part of the body. Then focus on relaxing and breathing.
- ☐ Lie down and imagine each part of your body is really heavy, sinking into the floor/bed/sofa. Breathe slowly and relax.
- ☐ Prayer, meditation or using your own spiritual beliefs
- ☐ Do you have a favorite relaxation technique?

Distracting Activities

What can we do when it's not possible to have quiet time? Sometimes we need passive distractions that enable us to turn off our thoughts, or at least drown them out for a while.

- ☐ Watch TV or a movie (see page 64)
- ☐ Listen to music (see page 63)
- ☐ Write in a journal (like now!)
- ☐ Paint or draw
- ☐ Write poetry or a song
- ☐ Sit in nature, listen to birds, and feel the breeze, sun or rain
- ☐ Talk to a friend
- ☐ Read a book (see your list on page 64)
- ☐ Go for a walk somewhere quiet and relaxing
- ☐ Play a video game
- ☐ Make a phone call
- ☐ Play a board game or cards

What works for you?

Come up with your own activities on the next page.

My Quiet Activities – Mind Map

(Write, draw or mind-map here)

Add some quiet activities to your safety plan

More About Me

Places I Like

(Write, draw or mind-map here)

Bedroom
Stables
Tigers
        Woodies
  Grandmas
        Matturn Fest
The Shed

Put these in your safety plan

Music That Makes Me Feel Good

Put some music in your plan

Artist	Song	Album
	Bangers N Mash	
Stormzy	Shut up	
Dave	Funky Friday	
Dave	Tiago Silver	
Dizzy rascal	Bonkers	

Books/ TV Shows / Movies I Like

On my block
sex education
~~so~~ friday night dinner.

Are any of these good for your plan?

How I Express Happiness & Excitement

Dance randomly

Add some to your plan

Chill Time

Amaze yourself!

Build an Emotional Thermometer

What's an Emotional Thermometer?

Building an emotional thermometer is about recognizing the things affect you, so you can plan strategies that help. It can be hard work looking at some of this stuff, so you may want to do this work with someone you can trust, instead of on your own.

Take your time. It can take weeks, months or only hours. It depends what you're ready for and how much work you've already done on the cause of your depression.

Whatever you do, remember this is not a test. It's a tool designed to help you figure out what works for you.

An emotional thermometer gives you a system for measuring your feelings of anxiety, depression or despair, and analyzing what is happening to you. If you share this with your therapist and someone you trust, then you both have a system for measuring your mood.

An emotional thermometer consists of

- ☐ Feelings
- ☐ Scales for measuring feelings
- ☐ Triggers
- ☐ Hazards
- ☐ Things that help
- ☐ Action you can take

Scales for measuring feelings

Our feelings can fluctuate. Measuring them on a consistent scale helps us, and the people we love, to evaluate where we are at. Sometimes it's hard to measure everything we're feeling on one scale, so a few scales to measure different aspects of our feelings can help.

An example: One teen measures himself on 3 scales.
- How strong are my negative thoughts? Or how loud?
- How well can I manage myself today?
- How willing am I to act on bad thoughts?

What could work for you? Choose **1 to 3 scales**. Any more can get hard to keep track of:
-
-
-

Any other ideas?
-
-
-

His scoring system:
- 1-3: Really good
- 3-5: Average
- 5-7: Stressful, but manageable.
- 7-8: Getting really uncomfortable & should let someone know.
- 8-8.5: Need to let people know immediately.
- 8.5-9: Dangerous. Implement safety plan with help from an adult.
- 9-10: Needs to be in the strict care of a responsible adult.

When he is scoring above 7 in all three areas, people need to keep an eye on him. Above 8 he's in distress. Above 8.5, he shouldn't be alone and should implement his safety plan immediately, with help from a parent, friend, teacher or counselor.

His trusted people know that if he scores 8 for negative thoughts, but his willingness to act on his thoughts is only 3, then he's in a much different situation than when all 3 scales are screaming 9 at him.

You scales may look different. Your emergency may be a 1, and 10 may be a great day. Your scale may go to 100 or 50 or even 1000. Do what makes sense to you.

Your Scoring System

Have a play with designing your scale and scoring system here.

In the More Resources section, there are Mood Logs, which let you rate yourself on a daily basis over a few weeks. This will help you see what affects you (pg 127).

What affects you?

Situations to avoid

When you're not feeling good, there are particular situations which could plunge you into despair or make you feel a lot worse. Part of managing yourself is to identify what situations affect you and try to avoid those, where possible.

Hazards & Triggers

Triggers are events or things that you associate with strong negative feelings. Think of these as things that increase your anxiety. Some people are terrified of dogs, others hate swimming pools, loud trucks or doors slamming. What causes you to feel anxious or stressed?

Remember, we're talking about things that have an extreme effect on you. Some situations are stressful for everyone, e.g.: most people don't like exams, but exams may be a trigger for you if they set off panic attacks. There's space on the next page to brainstorm what your triggers and hazards are.

Creating Your Emotional Thermometer

Your emotional thermometer measures your emotional health. Sharing it with the people you care about helps them know how you're doing, at a glance. If you tell them you're a 5/100, when 0 is the lowest you can be, then they know it's an emergency. If you're a 50/100 then they know you're having a bleh day, but it's not as bad as it could be.

Your emotional thermometer is made up of:
- your scales
- how they relate to you (what the scores mean)
- hazards and triggers
- your favorite 'go to' strategies that help

It could look like a thermometer (page 73-75), a graph, or a picture. It's up to you.

Triggers & Hazards List

Example: Emotional Thermometer

This is one teen's thermometer. In reality it's also full of color.

Hazards & triggers	Mood	What helps?
yelling	100%	safety plan & respite care
criticism		
storms	80%	family/friends bike / trampoline
mean gossip		memory jar
crowds	50%	sticky note wall sing / dance sensory box
dogs	30%	

73

Another Emotional Thermometer

Another teen created this thermometer.

The triggers and actions have been deleted.

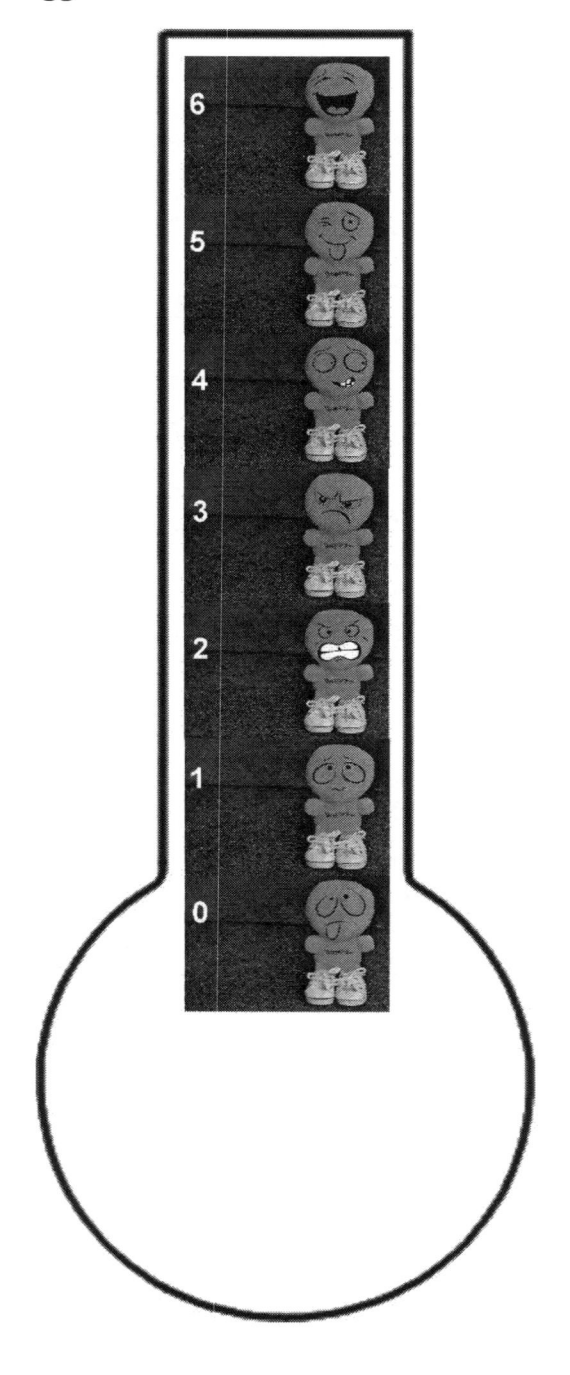

My Emotional Thermometer

Hazards & triggers   Scales   What Helps?

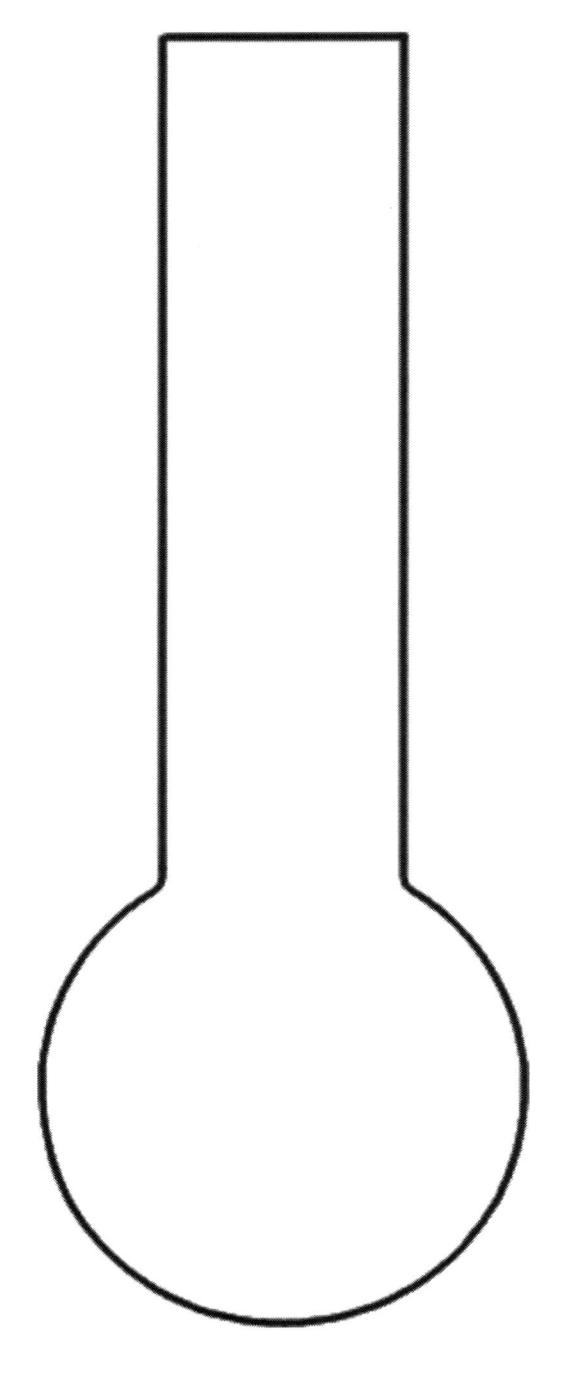

Fun Page - Your Own Design

Thermometer, graph, weather pattern—whatever suits you.
Design your own scale and system to measure your moods.

If you need a break, go to More Resources and do a maze, puzzle or coloring in page.

Build a Sensory Box

Build a Sensory Box

A sensory box is a valuable tool which utilizes all your different senses to calm you down or distract you when you're feeling anxious or stressed. You can start a collection at any time.

Step 1: Find a shoebox or another box with a lid and decorate it however you want.

Step 2: Collect, buy or make safe objects that you like to play with. (Please don't include any objects with sharp surfaces or that could be harmful.)

Tip 1: Try to include things that stimulate a variety of senses: sight, touch, smell, taste, hearing.
- Smell: relaxing scents
- Taste: sharp tastes are great for distracting us from distressing emotions
- Touch: textures that are soothing e.g.: fluffy, squishy, fuzzy, smooth, soft
- Sounds: cute sounds that you enjoy, favorite music
- Sight: colors you like, pleasing shapes, things that make you happy

Tip 2: Start small. A trip into your garden to pick a fragrant flower, a cool-looking leaf, a smooth stone and a soft dandelion head will start your box.

Step 3: Below are some cool items from other people's sensory boxes. Tick or circle the objects you'd like, then add some more.

- ☐ Slime
- ☐ Mini puzzles (plastic number slide puzzles, Sudoku, word finds, jigsaws)
- ☐ Play dough
- ☐ Rubber bands
- ☐ Glitter
- ☐ Pom-poms
- ☐ Whiteboard markers

- ☐ Mini whiteboard
- ☐ Glow in the dark stars
- ☐ Glow sticks
- ☐ Stickers
- ☐ Hacky sacks
- ☐ Magnets
- ☐ Stretchy rubber toys
- ☐ Twisty plastic toys
- ☐ Twisty plastic bracelets
- ☐ Strings of beads
- ☐ Kosh balls
- ☐ Knuckle bones
- ☐ Rattles
- ☐ Stress balls
- ☐ Small soft toys
- ☐ Crayons
- ☐ Bouncy balls
- ☐ Sticky notes
- ☐ Feathers
- ☐ Smooth stones
- ☐ Fake gemstones
- ☐ Tiny smooth pinecones
- ☐ Squeaky toys
- ☐ Herbs: rosemary, lavender, thyme, basil, mint
- ☐ Essential oils or perfume on cotton wool in plastic containers
- ☐ Ball bearings
- ☐ Rubik's cubes, or similar puzzles

- ☐ Strong tasting sweets (use sparingly: sherbet sticks; sour drops, breath mints)
- ☐ Bubble mixture
- ☐ Scraps of fabric of various textures e.g.: polar fleece, satin, sheepskin, leather, lycra, cotton
- ☐ Marbles of assorted colors
- ☐ Short piece of rope, only 2-3 inches long (rough texture, but not harmful)
- ☐ Cotton wool
- ☐ Soft earplugs (to block out sounds you don't like)
- ☐ Fidget spinners, fidget cubes or fidget pads

What now?

Have fun making your own list & mind map on the next pages.
Go outside and collect soothing things from your garden or a park to start your sensory collection. Oh, and don't forget to find a box and enjoy decorating it.

Things for My Sensory Box – Mind Map

(Write, draw or mind-map your items here)

FIDGET SPINNER x10

Things for My Sensory Box — List

Be a Warrior

Being True to Yourself

It's really important to be true to ourselves, but it's also important to help keep ourselves safe and to express our emotions safely. Lashing out at the source of our anger may harm ourselves or others. There are safe ways to express anger.

Being a warrior is about being able to express who you are in a way that's safe for you and others. It's about connecting with your emotions and expressing them, without hurting anyone. Especially not yourself. Especially not those who care about you. Or anyone else.

Squashing our emotions down, suppressing them or hiding them damages our mental health. Feeling sad or angry is a part of life. Being a warrior means expressing your true emotions safely.

See Creating Active Experiences on page 54-56 to find ideas for how to express your emotions safely.

Over the page, you have a chance to look at what things make you sad or angry and how you can express yourself without hurting anyone. Then you can design a warrior shield that suits you.

Things that Make Me Sad

Safe Ways I Can Express Sadness

Add some of these to your plan

Things that Make Me Angry

Safe Ways I Can Express Anger

Add some of these to your plan

Saying Yes and No

Life can be tough, with lots of people asking us to do things we're not okay with. This is an exercise that helps teenagers to decide what they do and don't want to do. It's another step in being true to yourself and being a warrior.

Each morning, decide you're going to say 'yes' to three things you really want and 'no' to three things you really don't want to do. You don't have to decide what the things are, but as the day goes on, be mindful of your decisions.

If someone asks you to join them for something that you're not keen on, say 'no'. If there's something you really want to do, but some of your friends don't want to, say 'yes' and do it. At the end of each day, review your 'yes' and 'no' decisions.

You may find it hard at first, especially if you're used to trying to please others, but keep practicing—it will get easier.

This exercise helps increase your self esteem and gives you a sense of control. If you want to write down your yes and no decisions each day, this may help you see your progress.

Note: Do not say yes to anything harmful (alcohol, drugs, smoking, self harm, fighting etc). Do not say 'no' if it will get you into major trouble (e.g.: skipping school).

Over the page you can make lists of things you enjoy or don't enjoy. This might help you make a few decisions about everyday things you can do or drop, to make you happier.

Everyday Things I Don't Like

(Cross out unnecessary tasks)

Everyday Things I Like

(Tick or circle the things you really love)

Warrior Shields

Warriors use shields to protect themselves. Often these are full of symbols that give warriors courage. The shield below has a bright star of hope at the centre and a raging fire which protects the warrior from attacks. The edge contains further symbols of two warriors standing back to back to fight off enemies, and another symbol of two hands clasped together in friendship. Color the shield, and then design your own.

My Warrior Shield

Draw and color your own Warrior Shield, full of cool things that make you feel safe. Use your favorite colors and the lists of safe activities and things you love. Over the page, you can design another shield of your own shape.

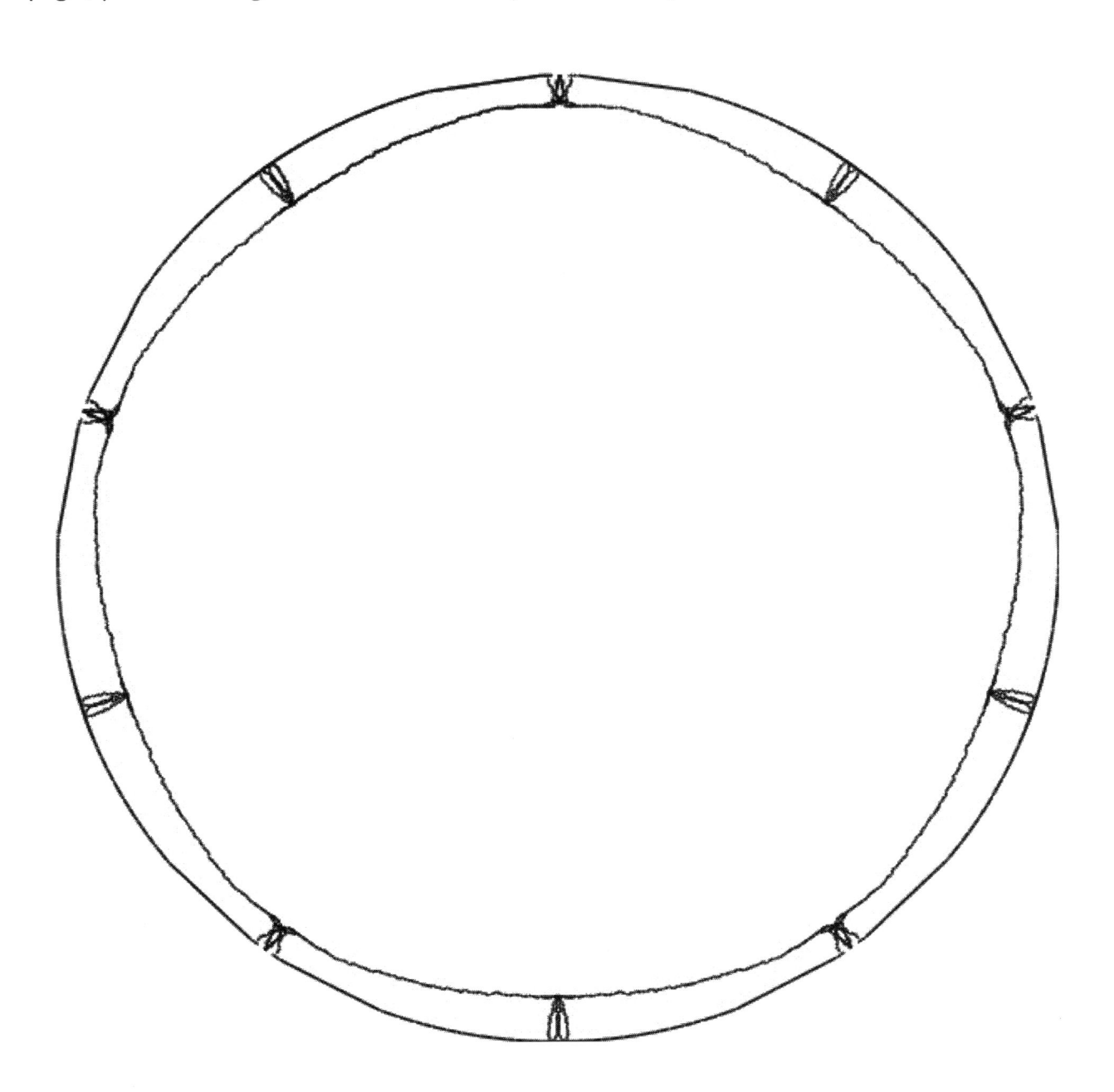

Design your own shield from scratch

Any shape, color or flavour you like!

My Treasure Chest of Memories

What's a Treasure Chest of Memories?

You can create a treasure chest full of special memories that you can enjoy when times are tough. You can call it what you want—a splendid moment jar, a good times treasury, special memories box, cool moments... whatever you like,

Step 1: Materials

- Container, jar, or box made of safe materials. E.g.: cardboard box, plastic carafe or jar, journal etc. You could even use this workbook!
- Brightly-colored paper
- Photos of fun times (optional)
- Cool mementos or cards & letters etc from friends (optional)

Step 2: Method

1. Record your favorite memories or fun times on colorful pieces of paper. You could write, draw or cartoon them.
2. Add them to your treasure chest / container / workbook.
3. As people give you compliments, write them down and add them too.
4. If you have some fun or share a joke with someone, add that to your chest.
5. You could write poems or songs or take photos. Whatever works best for you.

Step 3:

The following pages can help you get started until you have paper and a container. Brainstorm here. Make a collage, draw or stick photos in. Do whatever you like, as long as it's positive. Add something new each day, if possible. If you're finding it hard, brainstorm with a friend. Or notice the beautiful small things around you.

Step 4:

When you're sad, play music that makes you happy and look at these.

Nice Things That Have Happened Lately

My Favorite Memories

(Photos, drawings, writing, mementos etc)

Cool Times with Friends

Just For Fun

Color me brightly!

Build a Sticky Note Wall

What's a Sticky Note Wall?

Keeping It Positive

One teen I know covered his bedroom wall with hundreds of sticky Post-it notes. He had chronic depression and found it hard to keep going. During the day, at school or home, he wrote inspirational quotes from songs, books, TV shows, movies, memes, and even cool things friends said, on sticky Post-it notes.

Each night, he added them to his wall and watched it grow.

Each morning, he read one or two to start the day. He had a lot of negative thoughts bouncing round his head. He liked his sticky note wall for a few reasons.

"It helps me notice cool things in the day. It's bright and colorful and makes my room look happier. There are so many cool messages there from my favorite bands, from cool people I've met, and from my friends. When it's too hard to think of anything happy, my wall does it for me."

Feed yourself with positive messages that have meaning for you. Brainstorm over the next few pages. You can use these pages as your sticky note wall, or you can make a wall at home or use a journal.

If you're stuck, ask a friend to help you find some hopeful quotes. Search for inspirational quotes online. Choose quotes that have meaning for you. This is about what helps you. It doesn't have to happen all at once.

Start with one note.

That's how my friend started. You can do this.

Lyrics / Quotes that Mean Something

Qualities I Like About Myself

Glasses
Good fwend
Kind
fashion sense
taste in music

Things I'm Good At

HR
Running
Piano
PE
Revision
fast replies
being a v-good friend
streaks.
TikTok

Cool Things Others Say About Me

Cool Things I Say About Others

Saying positive things to other people can increase your self esteem. Setting a goal to say something nice to friends every day, may help you feel better. Try it, you might like it.

Chill Time

How about a moment to help save our planet? You could try volunteering for a cause you're passionate about. Or you could just do this word find.

```
O L A O I I N A L E G K V A
H A Z A R D O U S W A S T E
A Z W A L K I N G L D E N V
L E L I O W T E O V L E E A
A O G L O B A L O C R R M N
S A T Y I R V L Y G W T N P
T Y E K T P R C Y L E L O O
C P I H O T E N Y O U L R O
O N A W A R S T N A L P I L
G O E A S O N I C U K A V A
V R E T A W O K T V I R N I
L O E X E R C I S E S U E R
I V R E K N O S M R R L A E
O T P H N N I G V W S O E K
```

AIR
BIKING
CONSERVATION
EARTH
ENERGY
ENVIRONMENT
EXERCISE
GLOBAL
PLANTS
POLLUTION
POWER
RECYCLE
REUSE
SOLAR
TREES

HAZARDOUS WASTE
WALKING
VANPOOL

GREEN
WATER

Work Your Plan

You Can Do This

There are a lot of activities in this book. No one expects you to do everything, but hopefully you can find some tools that work for you. Do whatever helps.

Remember:
- Get help.
- Understand what affects you.
- Develop a scale so you can tell others how you're feeling. Tell them.
- Take care of yourself – sleep, eat well and take care of the basics (tough when you're depressed, but do what you can. No one expects you to be perfect).
- Figure out what strategies help you cope:
    - How to calm yourself
    - How to release energy when you're uptight
    - How to express hard emotions safely
    - How to distract yourself when things get tough
- Fill in the plan at the front of the book.
- Work your plan. Use it when times are tough.
- Rely on those you trust.
- Share your precious journey with someone you trust.

A teen staying at a youth mental health unit in a hospital recently told me this:

"Underneath the school desks is loads of graffiti. There's this one girl who kept coming back to the unit. No one wrote over her graffiti. She dated her stuff. The first thing she wrote was, 'The minute I get out of here, I'm going to kill myself.' Her next entry read, 'I'm back and I'm still alive, but I hate life.' Later she wrote, 'Things aren't as bad as I thought.' A year later, her friend wrote, 'She's out there. She's making it & she's never coming back, coz she's happy. I'm gonna do the same.'"

There are loads of teens out there battling depression, a day at a time. You can make it. Just hang in there and keep going. You can do this, one step at a time. One day at a time. One minute at a time. I hope this book helps you on your journey.

Trust someone. Reach out and get help. There <u>are</u> people who understand.

Tracking Progress

My Mood Log

Date	Day	Menstruating?	Hours of sleep last night?	Exercise?	Circle all your emotions	Best Score	Worst Score	What happened today?
					☹ 😐 ☺			
					☹ 😐 ☺			
					☹ 😐 ☺			
					☹ 😐 ☺			
					☹ 😐 ☺			
					☹ 😐 ☺			
					☹ 😐 ☺			
					☹ 😐 ☺			
					☹ 😐 ☺			
					☹ 😐 ☺			
					☹ 😐 ☺			
					☹ 😐 ☺			

How Was Today?

By tracking factors that may affect you, you'll find patterns

How Was Today?

Date	Day	Menstruating?	Hours of sleep last night?	Exercise?	Circle all your emotions	Best Score	Worst Score	What happened today?
					☹ 😐 ☺			
					☹ 😐 ☺			
					☹ 😐 ☺			
					☹ 😐 ☺			
					☹ 😐 ☺			
					☹ 😐 ☺			
					☹ 😐 ☺			
					☹ 😐 ☺			
					☹ 😐 ☺			
					☹ 😐 ☺			
					☹ 😐 ☺			
					☹ 😐 ☺			

Date	Day	Menstruating?	Hours of sleep last night?	Exercise?	Circle all your emotions	Best Score	Worst Score	What happened today?
					☹ 😐 ☺			
					☹ 😐 ☺			
					☹ 😐 ☺			
					☹ 😐 ☺			
					☹ 😐 ☺			
					☹ 😐 ☺			
					☹ 😐 ☺			
					☹ 😐 ☺			
					☹ 😐 ☺			
					☹ 😐 ☺			
					☹ 😐 ☺			
					☹ 😐 ☺			

How Was Today?

Date	Day	Menstruating?	Hours of sleep last night?	Exercise?	Circle all your emotions	Best Score	Worst Score	What happened today?
					☹ 😐 ☺			
					☹ 😐 ☺			
					☹ 😐 ☺			
					☹ 😐 ☺			
					☹ 😐 ☺			
					☹ 😐 ☺			
					☹ 😐 ☺			
					☹ 😐 ☺			
					☹ 😐 ☺			
					☹ 😐 ☺			
					☹ 😐 ☺			
					☹ 😐 ☺			

My Medication History

Medicine	Start Date	Dose Time/s & How*	How I feel	Side Effects	Date Stopped Why?

* Note the dosage, when it should be taken and any special instructions, e.g.: take with food, or one hour before sleep etc.

My Medication History

Medicine	Start Date	Dose Time/s & How*	How I feel	Side Effects	Date Stopped Why?

* Note the dosage, when it should be taken and any special instructions, e.g.: take with food, or one hour before sleep etc.

Where I Am Now

Date:_____

		Low High
Mental	Mood:	1 2 3 4 5 6 7 8 9 10
Mental	Studies/School:	1 2 3 4 5 6 7 8 9 10
Mental	Being Creative:	1 2 3 4 5 6 7 8 9 10
Physical	Physical Health:	1 2 3 4 5 6 7 8 9 10
Physical	Time Outside:	1 2 3 4 5 6 7 8 9 10
Physical	Eating Habits:	1 2 3 4 5 6 7 8 9 10
Physical	Water Drinking:	1 2 3 4 5 6 7 8 9 10
Physical	Exercise:	1 2 3 4 5 6 7 8 9 10
Social	Family:	1 2 3 4 5 6 7 8 9 10
Social	Friends:	1 2 3 4 5 6 7 8 9 10
Social	Relationships:	1 2 3 4 5 6 7 8 9 10
Social	Having Fun:	1 2 3 4 5 6 7 8 9 10
Spiritual / Mental	My Purpose:	1 2 3 4 5 6 7 8 9 10
Spiritual / Mental	My Past:	1 2 3 4 5 6 7 8 9 10
Spiritual / Mental	My Present:	1 2 3 4 5 6 7 8 9 10
Spiritual / Mental	My Future:	1 2 3 4 5 6 7 8 9 10

Draw an arrow to show which direction things are moving.
This gives you a baseline for later.

Where I'd Like to Be

When? _____

		Low High
Mental	Mood:	1 2 3 4 5 6 7 8 9 10
	Studies/School:	1 2 3 4 5 6 7 8 9 10
	Being Creative:	1 2 3 4 5 6 7 8 9 10
Physical	Physical Health:	1 2 3 4 5 6 7 8 9 10
	Time Outside:	1 2 3 4 5 6 7 8 9 10
	Eating Habits:	1 2 3 4 5 6 7 8 9 10
	Water Drinking:	1 2 3 4 5 6 7 8 9 10
	Exercise:	1 2 3 4 5 6 7 8 9 10
Social	Family:	1 2 3 4 5 6 7 8 9 10
	Friends:	1 2 3 4 5 6 7 8 9 10
	Relationships:	1 2 3 4 5 6 7 8 9 10
	Having Fun:	1 2 3 4 5 6 7 8 9 10
Spiritual / Mental	My Purpose:	1 2 3 4 5 6 7 8 9 10
	My Past:	1 2 3 4 5 6 7 8 9 10
	My Present:	1 2 3 4 5 6 7 8 9 10
	My Future:	1 2 3 4 5 6 7 8 9 10

Where I Am Now

Date:_____

		Low High
Mental	Mood:	1 2 3 4 5 6 7 8 9 10
	Studies/School:	1 2 3 4 5 6 7 8 9 10
	Being Creative:	1 2 3 4 5 6 7 8 9 10
Physical	Physical Health:	1 2 3 4 5 6 7 8 9 10
	Time Outside:	1 2 3 4 5 6 7 8 9 10
	Eating Habits:	1 2 3 4 5 6 7 8 9 10
	Water Drinking:	1 2 3 4 5 6 7 8 9 10
	Exercise:	1 2 3 4 5 6 7 8 9 10
Social	Family:	1 2 3 4 5 6 7 8 9 10
	Friends:	1 2 3 4 5 6 7 8 9 10
	Relationships:	1 2 3 4 5 6 7 8 9 10
	Having Fun:	1 2 3 4 5 6 7 8 9 10
Spiritual / Mental	My Purpose:	1 2 3 4 5 6 7 8 9 10
	My Past:	1 2 3 4 5 6 7 8 9 10
	My Present:	1 2 3 4 5 6 7 8 9 10
	My Future:	1 2 3 4 5 6 7 8 9 10

Draw an arrow to show which direction things are moving.
This gives you a baseline for later.

Where I'd Like to Be

When? _____

		Low High
Mental	Mood:	1 2 3 4 5 6 7 8 9 10
	Studies/School:	1 2 3 4 5 6 7 8 9 10
	Being Creative:	1 2 3 4 5 6 7 8 9 10
Physical	Physical Health:	1 2 3 4 5 6 7 8 9 10
	Time Outside:	1 2 3 4 5 6 7 8 9 10
	Eating Habits:	1 2 3 4 5 6 7 8 9 10
	Water Drinking:	1 2 3 4 5 6 7 8 9 10
	Exercise:	1 2 3 4 5 6 7 8 9 10
Social	Family:	1 2 3 4 5 6 7 8 9 10
	Friends:	1 2 3 4 5 6 7 8 9 10
	Relationships:	1 2 3 4 5 6 7 8 9 10
	Having Fun:	1 2 3 4 5 6 7 8 9 10
Spiritual / Mental	My Purpose:	1 2 3 4 5 6 7 8 9 10
	My Past:	1 2 3 4 5 6 7 8 9 10
	My Present:	1 2 3 4 5 6 7 8 9 10
	My Future:	1 2 3 4 5 6 7 8 9 10

Safety Plan

When I feel desperate, I'll talk to or be with (from pages 34 or 38)

_____ Phone:_____

_____ Phone:_____

_____ Phone:_____

Places I can be safe (from page 62):

_____

_____

_____

Things I'll do (including things from: quiet activities, pgs 58-60; active experiences, pgs 54-56; friends, pgs 34, 38; things you like to do, pg 45; safe things you can do if you're angry or sad pgs 86, 88).

_____

_____

_____

_____

_____

Things I'll take with me (including: sensory box, pgs 78-82; treasure chest of memories, pgs 96-99; this workbook; favourite distractions, pg 64; music, pg 63; food, pg 40-41; phone; medication pg 15 etc):

_____

_____

_____

Other Safe Ideas:

Safety Plan

When I feel desperate, I'll talk to or be with (from pages 34 or 38)

_____ Phone:_____

_____ Phone:_____

_____ Phone:_____

Places I can be safe (from page 62):

_____

_____

_____

Things I'll do (including things from: quiet activities, pgs 58–60; active experiences, pgs 54–56; friends, pgs 34, 38; things you like to do, pg 45; safe things you can do if you're angry or sad pgs 86, 88).

_____

_____

_____

_____

_____

Things I'll take with me (including: sensory box, pgs 78-82; treasure chest of memories, pgs 96-99; this workbook; favourite distractions, pg 64; music, pg 63; food, pg 40-41; phone; medication pg 15 etc):

_____

_____

_____

_____

Other Safe Ideas:

Another Word Find

Have fun with this happy-themed word find.
Thinking about happy words can make us feel a little lighter.
Try it and see if it works!

```
U P B E A T C H I R P Y
H A P P Y D R Y L L O J
J S C H E E R F U L G O
O E A G P L A G U A B B
Y R F N D O T H N U E P
N E U I R V I E G G L I
J N N S E E V E L H I L
T D P E A C E L A T E U
H I F A M S A G D E V F
G P U O I N S P I R E Y
I I S U N N Y E P O H A
L T A D E T A L E S I L
P Y D C I T A T S C E P
```

INSPIRE	SERENDIPITY	JOLLY
BELIEVE	CREATIVE	JOY
ECSTATIC	CHEERFUL	CHIRPY
LAUGHTER	PLAYFUL	PEACE
		DREAM
		LOVE
		ELATED
		FUN
		GLAD
		GLEE
		HAPPY
		HOPE
		SING
		SUNNY
		UPBEAT
		LIGHT

More Resources

Online Resources

There are a wide range of resources online:

http://www.nhs.uk/conditions/depression/Pages/Introduction.aspx

http://www.healthline.com/health/depression/exercise#1

http://teenmentalhealth.org/

https://www.mentalhealth.org.nz/get-help/a-z/resource/14/depression-youth

https://www.helpguide.org/articles/depression/teenagers-guide-to-depression.htm

http://www.walshinstitute.org/will-new-brain-biochemistry-findings-clear-the-murky-waters-of-depression.html

https://www.getselfhelp.co.uk/defusion.htm

https://www.youtube.com/watch?v=kwlYXupjoaI

https://www.youtube.com/watch?v=rCp1l16GCXI

http://www.healthtalk.org/young-peoples-experiences/depression-and-low-mood/topics

http://www.pbs.org/wnet/cryforhelp/featured/resources-hotlines-and-web-sites-for-teens/11/

http://trauma-recovery.ca/impact-effects-of-trauma/fight-flight-freeze-responses/

https://www.theguardian.com/childrens-books-site/2015/jan/01/top-10-teen-books-to-save-your-life-jennifer-niven

https://www.theguardian.com/culture/2017/jul/19/arts-can-help-recovery-from-illness-and-keep-people-well-report-says?CMP=fb_gu

Emotional Thermometer

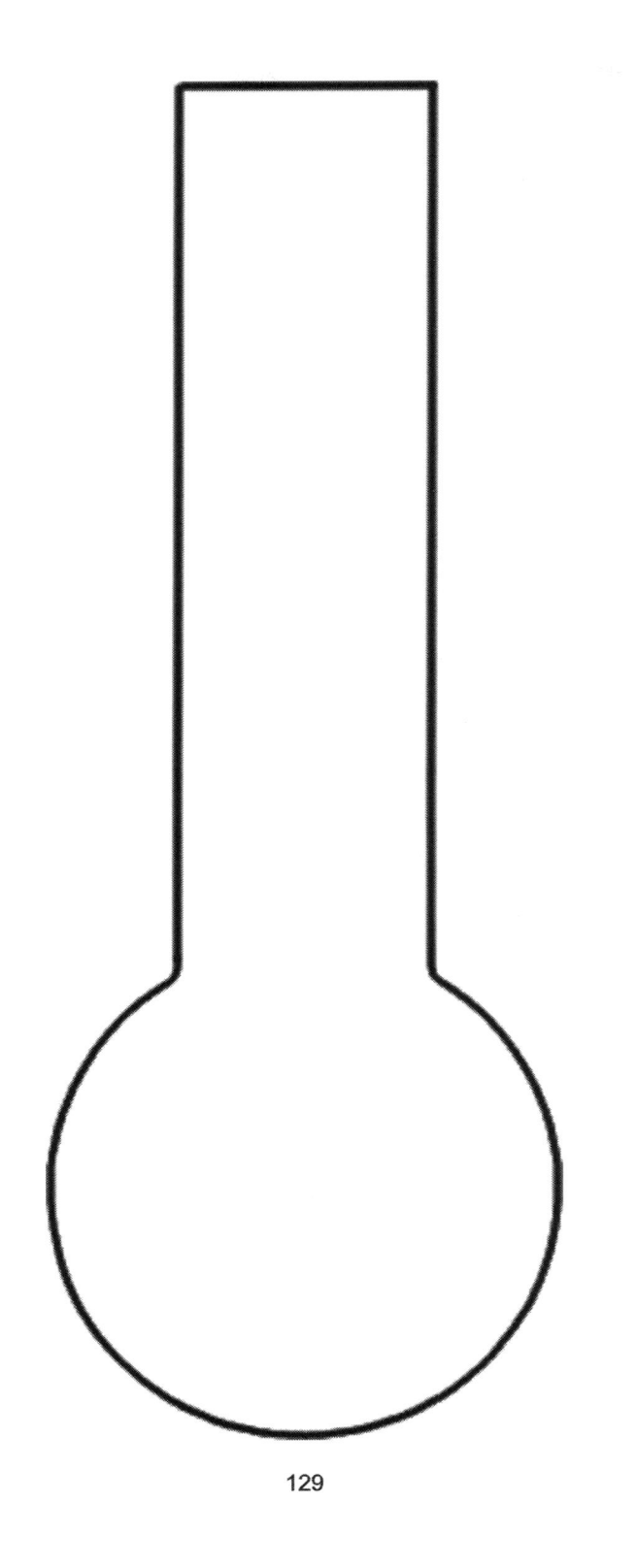

More Coloring Pages

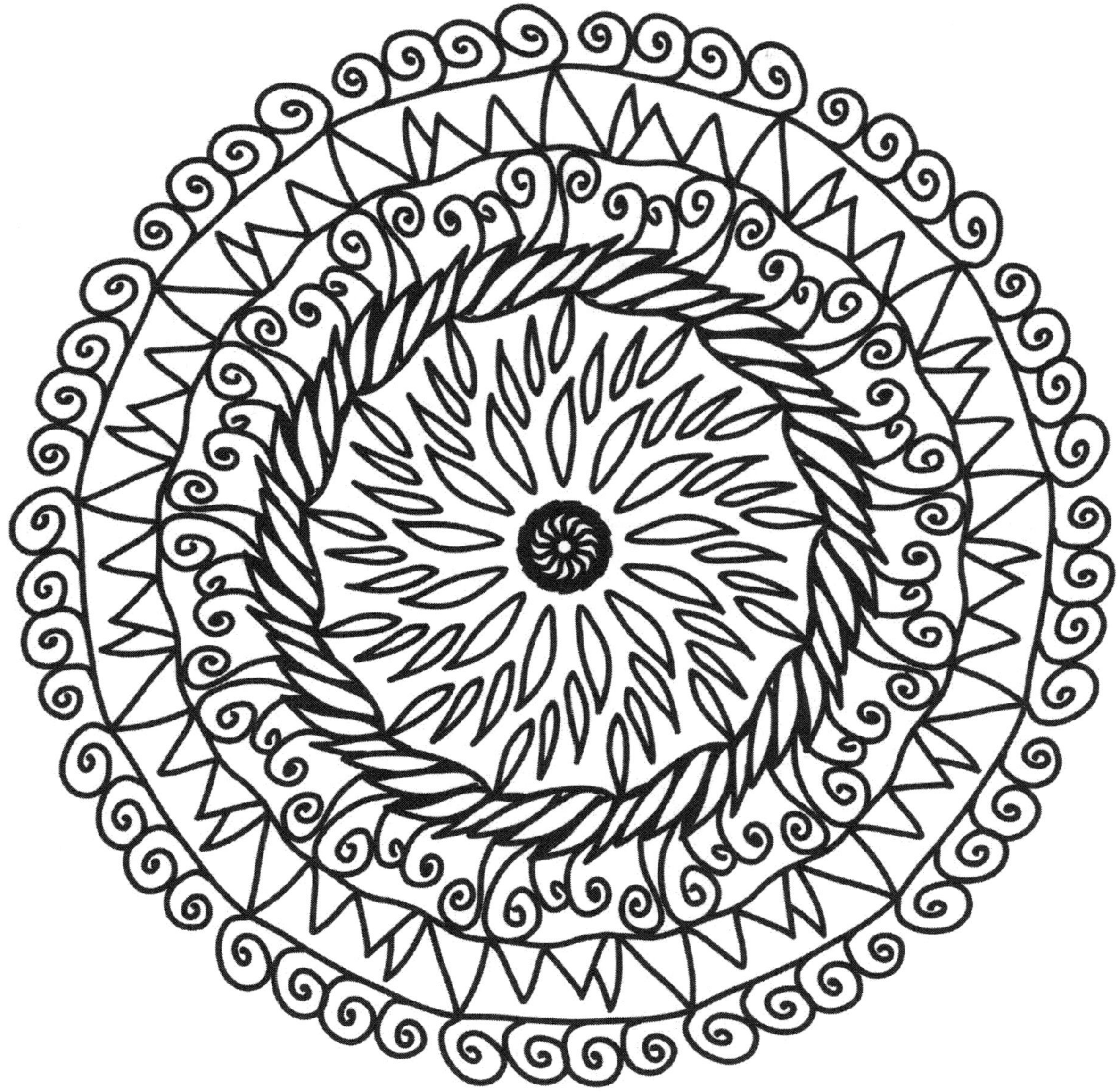

More Sudoku

	1	2		3	4	5	6	7
	3	4	5		6	1	8	2
		1		5	8	2		6
		8	6					1
	2				7		5	
		3	7		5		2	8
	8			6		7		
2		7		8	3	6	1	5

					3		8	5
		1		2				
			5		7			
		4				1		
	9							
5							7	3
		2		1				
				4				9

Another Maze

Good Luck and Good Planning

Having depression is not easy.

Hopefully, these tools, therapy and medical help will assist you on your road to recovery. It takes time. You're reprogramming your brain, learning coping techniques and new ways of looking at things. Planning and preparing strategies for bad days is a valuable part of taking control.

You may have setbacks or really bad days. Everyone has these. Reach out and ask for help. There are people around you that care, even though, at times, it doesn't feel that way.

Sometimes recovery feels like it's taking forever, but you will get there. There will be days when you feel stuck, but hang in there. Use some of the tools we've examined. Stick to your safety plan. Reach out to a friend, go to a safe place, and take safe things to do to occupy yourself.

If that doesn't work, or you're feeling really desperate, call a hotline or go to the nearest hospital for help.

Things will get better. Depression is manageable. Many people recover from it. Remember the girl who graffitied under the desk? (Page 110). She didn't want to live. She couldn't imagine living through more pain. But she made it and she's been an inspiration to others who are struggling too. Please be patient with yourself. You deserve all the love you can get, especially from you.

I wish you truckloads of luck on your journey, many happy moments and a bright future. A future of happiness—a different reality from what you're living now.

You are important. Fight to survive! You can do this, one step at a time.

Printed in Great Britain
by Amazon